The Bear Wrestler

Robert Ostrom

Distributed by Independent Publishers Group
Chicago

©2025 Robert Ostrom

No part of this book may be used or reproduced in any manner without written permission except in the case of brief quotations embodied in critical articles and reviews. Please direct inquiries to:

Saturnalia Books
2816 North Kent Rd.
Broomall, PA 19008
info@saturnaliabooks.com

ISBN: 978-1-94781-77-84 (print), 978-1-94781-77-91 (ebook)
Library of Congress Control Number: 2024948729

Book design by Robin Vuchnich
Cover art by Nathan Ng Catlin

Distributed by:
Independent Publishing Group
814 N. Franklin St.
Chicago, IL 60610
800-888-4741

FOR MY FATHER
ROBERT EARLE OSTROM

Contents

An Act of Preservation	9
A History of Bear Wrestling in the United States	21
At the Center of the Story Stands a Bear	55
The Cosmic Hunt	69
Instructions for Growing a Forest	79
Exit, Pursued by a Bear	95
Killing of the Sacred	107
The Bear Wrestler	117

While we were fearing it, it came,
But came with less of fear,
Because that fearing it so long
Had almost made it fair.

> Emily Dickinson

Risley kids and slanging buffers, Lord only knows how they suffers.

> Late 19th Century Circus Rhyme

when the wrestlers' sinews
grew long like metal strings,
he felt them under his fingers
like chords of deep music.

> Rainer Maria Rilke

what you come from is craziness, what your
mother and her mother come from is

craziness, panic of the animal
smelling what you have in store for it.

> Frank Bidart

The Bear Wrestler

his back
is aged leather
a clay map
of swells and knots
moles cherry spots
the sea still
and wet sands
at low tide a cluster
of black hair
is bluestem below
a cloud behind
his heart a key
in a seasonal river
borders his spine
the longest scar
I have ever seen
above it storied
like an empty
eye socket
a smaller scar

An Act of Preservation

1.

At the center
of the story
stands a father.

2.

Everything is as it was when I was a boy. The village, mountains, houses, the still-colorful petunias overflowing flower boxes on windowsills. There's the woman hanging laundry in her yard. A breeze bellows the sheets. Nearby, a shirtless man shovels coal from an open-top wagon.

3.

By his strength, his children will soar.

4.

There'd always been decay: a downed telephone pole, the billboard for slice and serve Baby Ruth tilting back, a lead scarecrow face-up in the garden. Something dug into the gravel at a rail junction, and a pigeon feather rests like a bridge across the acrylic lake.

5.

If stories are the hardtack of life, a ship sits in a harbor hidden by the fog of his childhood.

6.

Streetlamp over a birdbath, a robin perched on the lip. Despite the ruins, the detail is astounding. Towering over it, my girlfriend and I stand side-by-side in a hole cut in the middle. She points to a brakeman on top of a train. The tell-tale like a gallows above him.

7.

"Thou shalt have no other gods before me," the story goes.

8.

The model railway lives in the dry attic of a house my dad and his partner Tim converted into an assisted living facility or, as we call it, an old folks' home. I have brought her to my hometown to meet my family and see where I grew up, but for other reasons too, which are the same reasons I brought you here. Maybe these are the reasons the hobbyist built this place. Did he imagine us standing together, hovering like birds that won't ever come to rest?

9.

I remember him running
away the ring the ruse
the bear hug I remember
the hotdog stand I touch the scar

10.

There is the distinct feeling this workmanship preserves a collection of places in memory.

11.

After his mother died, my dad broke the law twice. Although her house had been sold months prior, following her death he snuck onto the property where he had spent his childhood and dug up her beloved rosebush. Then, he stole into Lakeview Cemetery, buried her ashes above my grandfather and planted the roses at their grave. He wore a suit as he did this work. It was herringbone. Years later, he buried the ashes of my younger sister in the same spot.

12.

The constructed world is also an attempt to correct something inside of its maker. Look at their faces, each hand-painted. All the people here—even those riding bikes, swimming, kayaking—their expressions are identical as though they've all suffered the same loss.

13.

All my life I have struggled with his lies. But how I love his stories.

14.

Interiors are even more meticulous than the outside world. Within an ivy-covered house a man sits at a desk, a milk glass lamp beside him. Through open chapel doors: seated parishioners witness a baptism. The cars are mostly 1930s Mercedes and Volkswagens. Grass sprouts through the cracks of a cement parking lot behind a factory. A woman, alone toward the end of the lot, seems to step backwards. Above her, a stone-lined tunnel runs through the brick chimney.

15.

Of his stories, my favorites were fablelike. While hauling groceries back to the trailer park, my dad takes a shortcut through the woods where he encounters a wild turkey blocking the trail. Instinctively, and not knowing how offensive these words are to turkeys, he says, "gobble, gobble." The bird attacks, dad drops his bags and as he's running, he glances back to see the turkey rummaging through the groceries. In another story, like an omen, he finds a furry tarantula crawling on his firstborn daughter in her crib. As I grew into an adolescent and therefore a skeptic, the bear wrestling story was the first to be catalogued as suspect, and I began to wonder if I was being lied to all the time.

16.

But a truth can also conceal a lie.

17.

I was ten when we moved into an old colonial that my dad bought to keep my mother from leaving. When she was a girl, it had been her favorite house with its weeping brick and white-shuttered windows. Though the house was still beautiful, urban blight had touched that part of the neighborhood which was probably why we could afford it. Worse yet, the people who lived there before us left an unsettling feeling about the place. Mom had it exorcised. That didn't make it any safer. Our fears materialized at bedtime. Some nights, the house was loud with screams from one or all three of my sisters while other nights it was loud with fighting. I was always too afraid to stay in my room. After my parents put a lock on their door, I would sleep on the bathroom floor until a ghost drew a bath and tried to drown me in the tub.

18.

Once, when my dad attempted to start it, the AC transformers sparked and smoked and we never tried again. Though I would've liked to see all the trains snake around at once, to watch the lights click on and the crane at the depot lift rocks into the air, the gestating world itself, a diorama, a dream, a prayer, was always enough. Above the tunnel, a hot air balloon hangs from a pulley in a rafter and under that, near the top of a tall Styrofoam mountain, a hunter trudges, his rifle resting on his shoulder. A few inches away from him, an elk grazes, but the hunter's dog sniffs in the other direction, toward denser woods. On the opposite face of the mountain, the base rolls into sand where, under a lighthouse, people sunbathe and wade in the ocean at the edge of the table. A child waves up to the ridge where the tracks curl past the shoreline. At the end of a pier reaching away from the scene, two figures sit. Their feet sway above the suitcases and hatboxes of residents whose families never gathered their belongings.

19.

The first false awakening I can remember because it happened so many times. The distance between me and my parents' bedroom is a wilderness. Outside my doorway, the staircase. A black bear stands at the bottom, and most nights I don't look at it, but sometimes I do. It is not menacing nor is it comforting. It seems to be waiting. I make a dash for my parents' room and pray the door isn't locked.

20.

Do all of his stories add up to a life story? This is the earliest one I can recall: when my dad was a little boy, he and another friend fashioned a parachute out of a vinyl tablecloth tied to a laundry basket. The friend lived on the top floor of a high-rise apartment building, so his kitchen window was their launching point. With basket and parachute perched on a windowsill, my dad climbed in, and before he could have second thoughts, his friend pushed him out of the window. My dad plummeted to the ground far below where he certainly would've been killed had it not been for a gust of wind that lifted him up into the air and over his neighborhood, the river, and downtown, until finally he got tangled on a flagpole at City Hall where he waited a long time before the fire department rescued him.

21.

When I was a teenager, one night after my mother had moved out, I woke and walked out of my room. As I passed the large hallway mirror, I saw I had no reflection.

22.

We crawl out to leave. By the push-button light switch, under knob-and-tube wiring, rest tools and piles of materials. Little bags with brands such as "Life-Like," "Natural Scale Scenics," and "Perma-Scene." Each bag is filled with something different: grass, stone, earth, lichen, modeling compound. A mouse chewed a hole into the autumn trees and the colors spill out beside an empty box of hardwood forest.

23.

Some of my fondest childhood memories took place in the community theater where my whole family would act in musicals. My dad continued to perform after all of us left. Not too long ago, he sent me a placard of himself as the lead in *Chicago*. It was an imitation of the theatrical release poster for the film. Instead of Richard Gere flanked by Renée Zellweger and Catherine Zeta-Jones, my dad stood between two young women. One thing that strikes me about the poster, other than the fact that he sent it to me, is that my dad is wearing his own suit and his hair is in the style that he's had for over fifty years. Come to think of it, his hair is the same for all of the characters he's played. It's as though he shapes them into his own image. For instance, as the Pirate King in *The Pirates of Penzance*, Dad was clean-shaven with his hair in a classic part. The second time he performed in *Oklahoma!*, when he played Curly, he allowed one curl to fall on his forehead. To me, this doesn't allow my dad to absorb his characters, but he sees it differently.

24.

Our three-year-old daughter is so obsessed with Disney's *Mulan* that we either have to refer to her as Mulan or more often, Mulan's male alter ego, Ping. She tells me a story about the young warrior defeating "bad boy Shan Yu" and the Huns, thus saving all of China and bringing honor to her family. I tell her, "What a great story!" She replies, "It's not a story, Dad. It's a plan."

25.

We walk down the narrow servants' stairwell that eventually leads to the kitchen. I pause to look out a window, half-expecting to see a giant man gazing into an eyeglass.

26.

He could throw a child higher than any parent dared to try. I remember lining up with neighborhood kids waiting to be thrown. Because he was so strong, he could do this even as we grew into adolescents. If I dig deep, I can still feel what it was like to fly so far into the air. At that height, the sky was full of names, but I was never up there long enough to say any of them. The fall was fast and perilous and it always ended in his arms.

27.

Before bed, when I sing, read, or make up a story for my children to fall asleep to, I know that I am creating an emotional memory, a pleasing experience that their brains will continue to seek for the rest of their lives. With so much influence over these people, how can I possibly not screw them up? More importantly, why did they choose me to be their dad?

28.

"Where was it one first heard of the truth? The the."

29.

One Thanksgiving after supper, my dad and I drove off from my grandparents' house in Waterford, PA, leaving behind my mom and sisters because we could care less about Black Friday at the Erie Mall. On our way home, we got caught in a blizzard and had to pull over to the side of the road. This is back when I-86 was Route 17, a slender two-way highway. We couldn't see anything until it was right on us. At one point, a gust of wind cleared the snow long enough for my dad and I to spot an overturned big rig across the road. In our white Pontiac Dustbuster parked by a guardrail, I sat with him, waiting for something to crash into us. The experience should've been terrifying but instead, Dad distracted me with jokes and stories as falling snow slowly buried our van. He told me how once, up near Lake Erie where I-86 curves into I-90, he watched a car fly off the embankment and land in a tree. The other story he told that night was about the time he was driving during a whiteout on this same road. Because the plows couldn't keep up with the storm, he was unable to see the blacktop and didn't realize that he'd driven miles off, deep into farmland.

30.

We pass through the pantry, the common areas, and then I show my girlfriend one of my favorite rooms—an addition built for a wealthy woman in the early 90s. She had recently passed, but we're surprised to find her bed still unmade with two small slippers on the floor. Inside one of the slippers stands her artificial leg. In the basement my dad has his office, and on the desk and shelves there are piles of old scratch-off tickets.

31.

Figure of the bear wrestler, surrounded by distance and snow.

32.

"I don't like fireworks, and I don't like Orion," my daughter declares as we stand under the stars in our new backyard. "They aren't really real," I try to explain to her. "A long time ago people gave names to shapes they saw in the stars. That's pretty much it." She's not listening but I go on, "They either invented stories to go with the shapes or the shapes became characters from stories they already told." The great bear walks above our building. "Well I don't like Orion," she repeats. As I stare into that vacant patch where the crab digs its claws in and looks at the bear, I think, *He's not hunting you.*

33.

What if you can kill a truth by telling a story?

34.

I've returned to believing my father truly did wrestle a black bear at a fair in Gary, Indiana in 1971.

A History of Bear Wrestling in the United States

The Ring Names of Bears

Alice Teddy	Bruno	Rene
Andy	Brutus	Rex
Battling Bruno	Buster Bruin	Sampson
Ben the Brute	Caesar	Smokey
Bess	Curley	Sonny
Betty	Gentleman Ben	Teddy
Big Andy	Ginger	Terrible Ted
Big Ben	Gorgeous Gus	Toby
Big Boy	Hercules	Tokyo Rose
Big Bruiser	Jiggs	Toto
Big Jim	Lena	Trotski
Billy the Bear	Leni	Trotsky
Bosco	Marian	Vic the Bruiser
Brownie	Markoff	Vicious Victor
Bruin	Martin	Victor
Bruiser Ben	Pete	Victor II

D. Boon cilled a bar in year 1760

when I was a meadow
they watered me
with blood now
I am dust that clouds
the air soon after
a crowd begins to cheer

The Diary of William Bentley 1798

hair flowing
and white
every
thing had
the depth
of winter
the drifts
on the neck
above knee
deep it was
hanging weather

Frontierland 1836

absent
a butcher
knife licked
a b'ar into
table meat
spun yarn
far as
the father
of waters
miles from
truth where
backyard
boys in
a hundred
years grin
down the ugly
dog digging
up bushes

Battling Bruno, Knight of the Royal Bath mid-19th Century

this desire to
rime with land
hooked me
by the mouth
dragged me back
made me a symbol
on the banner
for surrender

Les Montreurs d'ours d'Ercé 1870

I have learned
to sleep by pressing
my arm against
my ear where
I hear the river
loud across
the wilderness
of me it forms
a basin in my belly
and on the shore
beneath my fur
from where
I was tied
to my mother
a hemlock grows
tall wide weeping
I curl into her

Old Boy Martin 1871

often at night I fear
drunk he'll play
his spoons the barrel
music that fevers
the floor of my cage

Ursus Arctos 1871

a blue whale passes
under the brown
bear in its pen
in stowage

Théâtre Français, New York City 1877

she pulled my hair
gnawed my ears
and used every
artifice within
the range of her
sagacity to defeat me

The New York Times 1877

was given over
to wrestling
muscular Christians
of every order
and admirers of
muscular Christianity
in the abstract

Lena's Revenge 1878

the cause of death
fast living
and a Pyrenean bear

Woods Theater, Cincinnati 1878

the skins of drums
and bitten off thumbs
that's what little boys
are made of

The Inter-Ocean Traveling Curiosities of the 1880s

these lucrative concerts
of the tent the Double
Sex Wonder a walking
skeleton Ursa the Bear
Girl missing links
or dancing to the music
of a steam calliope
Circassian beauties
with beer-teased hair
the Pig Faced Woman
is a black bear shaved
and drunk in a day dress
ringlets and a bonnet Tom
Thumb at an electrocution
machine the Two-Headed
Nightingale with tangled
tresses sings *Die Schwestern*

Bess at Roger's Park, Chicago 1902

many skilled
in the difficult
half nelson

and on
intimate terms
with the choke

hold has gone
down
to the mat

beneath
the weight
of the bear

Orpheum Theater, Boston 1913

Big Jim vs all comers

Nick Lassa of the Oorang Indians National Football League Team 1922

I brought
with me
a coyote
muscle
history
once
in a while
we raised
a little
money
and all
of hell

Will You Miss Me When I'm Gone? Mervin Barackman 1930s

I dedicate this fight to Willette
my first wife love of my life
serving hard labor up the river
and to our son Jack who drowned
in Cottage Lake around 1928
my career in Physical Culture
was picking up steam I took
my rastling show my bears
from Spokane to Clovis back up
to the shore of Bitter Lake
Centralia to El Teatro Esperanza
Iris to Chico San Francisco
Vancouver Montgomery to Abilene
you see I don't stand still
well since I was a kid things going right
never quite moved me I suppose it's in
retribution where I'm most at peace
the morning after a fight I touch each
of my injuries with affection as if
the Lord Himself had kissed me from
the inside though once in Walla Walla
I earned a welt that looked like Willette's
mouth and I swear she whispered me
to sleep her voice the only weight
that can pin me breathless then

I was in the lake and she said
look how the water swims the fish
our animal shadows frolicked
below us as we lay down with Jackie
cutthroats reeling about our skin
above us algae bloomed into sky

Toto at the Shreveport Municipal Auditorium 1939

jeers and jibes
and roughshod rides
that's what little boys
are made of

Vermont State Fair 1943

with the backlight
I couldn't tell
the difference
between bear
and wrestler

Ada Ash ca. 1960

the closeness
of death
is not
marked
in inches
but in
beatings
or inside
his heavy
coat where
it's less
of a fall
and more
like flight
like being
thrown
I thought
I'd never
come
down

Terrible Ted 1963

in this life I am permitted only to pretend
and though he doesn't let me sleep much
under the porch in winter I sense the ice
below the mat then my mind runs far
enough from my body that the world
is nothing but a dream of flying mares
and strangles I've got this itch in me
a hankering whose roar grows more
distant and for this distance louder
every day is a freight train at and away

Gorgeous Gus 1964

the night a fight
from today
there's nothing
anyone can do
that will warm
from me
the winter

Adolphus "Tuffy" Truesdale 1970

my mother was an alligator
did I say mother I meant
I kept her in a tank under my
bed for years until I couldn't
take the dreams anymore
now from the back of our
luxurious lorry and cocktail
lounge a Chevy Impala airport
limousine tongue like a red
ribbon licking all over my ears
cauliflowered from ground
to fairground then auditorium
Paint Your Wagons
To Tell the Truth
and Let's Make a Deal
for your hedonistic mirth
the bear the heel will beat
the evermore meat out of Rowdy
Roddy Piper Superstar Billy Graham
or any slick-faced blowhard
in the stands my boy can take the hell
out of the devil's sails as he's done
formerly and will do after the bluster
the arm drags the cock-a-doodle-dos
the lariats and monkey flips after

a pitcher of martinis gorgeous fat
olives then I'm back on the mat
with the dead gator I try to growl
but it's a gurgle I can't
get the bear out of me

Gary, Indiana 1971

treed
by dogs
wind made
the sound
of hands
kneading
each other
branches
knuckles
cracking

Iowa State Fair 1972

I didn't
hear him
singing
I could
barely
smell him
under my
own panting

Fire on the Mountain late 1970s

man vs a stone
man vs hosta
woman vs a room of phantoms
alone vs alone with everyone
lady fern in June vs any green
stone vs a well

Matilda the Hun 1980s

to prove

I was one
of the boys

I fought a female
fanged and kept

on a leash she
could have broken

me but I lasted
some men

they want
to be squished

and live
inside you

Are the Good Times Really Over (I Wish a Buck Was Still Silver),
Tracy Smothers 1987

slather me
with honey
cattle prod
and turn
them loose
nothing scares
this wild-eyed
boy more than
his own cells
tumbling
through tissues
and organs
like snow
balls headed
for hell

Caesar 1996

the weather locked
in the last of us
so we stripped
down and dove
into thorn-filled
clouds from then
on everywhere I
touched was heat

At the Center of the Story Stands a Bear

The Original Word for Bear is Lost

The Ancestor
The Animal
Apple of the Forest
Arctic
Arctos
Arthur
Bar
Baer
The Barefooted One
The Beast
Beauty of the Forest
Bee Wolf
Beer
Beowulf
Bernadette
Bernhard
The Big Furry One
The Big One
Bjorn
Black Place
Blue Tail
Bodvar Bjarki
Brilliant
Broad Foot
The Brown One
Bruin
Bruno
Chief's Son

Cloudberry Boy
The Dark
Dark Thing
Destroyer
Destroyer of Beehives
The Divine One Who Rules the Mountains
The Dog of God
Father
Forest Apple
Fur-Robed Forest Friend
Garcia
Glory of the Forest
God
Golden Light Foot
The Good Calf
Grandfather
Grandmother
Great Man
Hairy
Harm
Honey Eater
Honey Master
Honey Paw of the Mountains
Honey Pig
Honey Thief
Injury
Keeper of Dreams
Keeper of Medicine

The Licker
Lightfoot
Long Hams
Man
Man of God
Master
Mead Paw
Meadow
Moss
Nita
Old Furred One
The Old Man with the Fur Coat
Old One of the Forest
The One that Hears Everything
The One that Sleeps in the Winter
The One that Walks with a Light Step
The One Who Licks with its Tongue
The One Who Owns the Chin
The One Who Owns the Den
The One Who Strikes and Kills
Orso
Ours
Owner of the Earth
The Pride of the Thicket
Pride of the Woodlands
Shaggy
Short Tail
Snub Nose

The Son of My Aunt
Sticky Mouth
The Strong One
Thick Haired One
The Unmentionable One
Ursula
Ursus
The Violent
Wide Brow

False Awakening

there is always a wind in this house

suckling claws newly sharpened blades

the carpet reserved for children and other

animals on the floral couch adults

laugh unaware of the danger it's going

to grow fast I want to say but before

I breathe to speak the pet has doubled in size

when it rips me open someone shouts look

he's blooming but they might've said burning

The Bear Wrestler

call him digging ditches
for living we eat for temper
drunk at the bar stole animals
on the road airport deer
followed him all day this dead
girl this guy covered in his pulse
to take a bath in a bear ago
finger in the scar the man in
the world came to Salvation
did dumb things raised my hand
and told him a liar you're
in the world because my dad
is in the world and all the kids
laughed at me and I screamed
a liar a liar and everyone quiet
looked and said oh wait I'm
sorry you're right I forgot he is
in the world his hands his hands
his hands thinking them together
sandpaper inside a shell his middle
finger a bald man that no one
takes seriously lost in my room
I think back but when I play
outside on the brown couch
stitching thread pushing a needle
through the open house and do
any of you think I'm getting

better I want to be a hall
when he got mad and stormed
I tried to stop him I punched him
in the gut he spun and fell
down I ran as fast as the boys
someday most boys grow up
it's a curse my grandma and I cried
when he died curly hair he looks
just like the basement upstairs
mirrors and family are all missing

He Smiles He Waves

From where he hangs, my father can see a far piece. Beneath him is the whole town. The wind rocks and turns him like a weathervane; it forces him to look north over the police station, the tan-brick high school, in the direction of the cemetery. Over his shoulder he sees Chautauqua Lake reflecting the sky. It's early spring. There's no ice on the water, but the feeling of ice in the air means no pleasure boats are out today. When a strong wind spins him fast, the Chadakoin River wraps his mind and he thinks of his father. So toward the Crescent Tool Factory he looks, hoping to catch him walking home from work. More likely he's at the bar, the one in the reeds near the tire piles, the one called The Swamp. Unwinding, my father slows and to the northwest thinks he sees Lake Erie but it's just a trick of the sky. He hears sirens growing louder, the firetruck shouldering its way. He turns again, and to the southeast sees the tiny homes on Swede Hill where he flew from only moments before. He looks down the hill to his house on the other side of the river, near where one day he'll crawl across the scaffold of the unfinished Washington Street Bridge. Is my mom home yet? he wonders. Now the fire department is raising a ladder. They've prepared the life net. Standing in a bushel basket tied to a nylon tablecloth, hanging from a flagpole, my father sees the crowd gathered below, looking up at him as if watching a comet.

Portrait of My Sister as Bear

her claws her black fur
cinnamon marked portrait
of my sister as canines
as meat and marrow
portrait of my sister
licking her cubs as her mother
licked her in the boreal forest
portrait of my sister
with breath sweet from fresh
berries and bugs how she loves
the rain portrait of my sister
as fog between mountains
she feels it on her nose
portrait of my little sister
with her leg in the jaws of a trap
her litter in a tree above her
portrait of my sister inside
a truck cage on I-80 the shake
and bang the compressor hissing
smell of asphalt roadkill a storm
twenty miles away portrait
of my sister muzzled mitted
defanged portrait of my sister
with arm and ankle tendons cut
portrait of my sister as beer-fueled
and egged-on portrait of her

holding a man he smells like mule
deer and grass portrait as victor
drinking a Coca-Cola portrait
of my sister sick and thinning
portrait of my sister dying
in the mud on the floor
of her cage how she loves the rain
and the mess it makes portrait
of my sister as pith in an incinerator
she will come back a spirit bear
music of her yearlings rolling in the soil
the pine needle the moss-covered earth

The Bear Wrestler

makes me wait in the car outside my girlfriend's house
sitting beside me in his wool overcoat
he's searching his pockets for a Fisherman's Friend
he calls them breath mints
he is his wool overcoat pockets full of leaves
he is his wool overcoat pockets full
of Fisherman's Friends buried in pipe tobacco loose change
he'll find me two dirty lozenges one for now and one for
his wool overcoat is dry grass under snow-wet leaves
he is his wool overcoat is a grainfield he wraps around me
he empties his pockets a ring falls out
then a house then a family
his overcoat contains every one of him
he says let's build ourselves a fire

The Bear Wrestler

Not like a pierce but a punch then I was a stranger. The news was mine first, it was a cut in my back and my words left me a river gushing. All those people handling my body was my initial worry. For a second I lost my legs. If I was caught, I'd be in deep shit back at the barracks and there was nothing I was more afraid of than the box. Bells, distant music, thrilled screams. Some people started toward me so to all fours I rolled over like an animal. I stayed and watched. I smelled hotdog steam and wondered if I was covered in it. I sniffed the collar of my summer whites. She was all over me, her scent I mean: pungent sweat even the stench of her breath. My arms buckled and I fell face-first into the concrete. Things got quiet and scattered all over, cans of pop and Old Style and hotdog wraps, then someone offered his hands. By the grace of God and a steel countertop, I pulled myself up. I looked at the audience. I smiled. I laid it on thick and you know my smile it took the wind out of them. I wanted to see what hurt me, maybe the counter of the hotdog stand but I couldn't find any blood—light didn't throw far in those days—then I spotted it dripping from a hand crank to the trailer latch and pooling on the cement. Let me tell you it's weird to see your life on the ground mixed in the dirt and trash in front of a crowd. Where were my brothers? Then these men in flannel with a plywood gurney. I half-thought I was already gone. I smiled again. I stopped those guys in their tracks. The whole place seemed to relax. With all the strength I could muster, I forced out a laugh and honest to God it's crazy but my laugh changed forever after that.

Third Class Swim Test

at the edge
of the story
stands a father
the story is filled
with water
and because
the father
doesn't know
how to swim
he eases in
and floats
the distance
takes
a lifetime

The Cosmic Hunt

Two Arrows

the first ripped through me
as if shot from above
entering my neck then
piercing a lung
and splintering into
my veins I was neither saint
nor fawn I wasn't even
a wild goose though I could
tell by the blood that the first
was a hunting arrow
you are the second

Although Many Saw a Bear

dog	ladle	alligator
canoe	sickle	prawn
saucepan	hog's jaw	shrimp
coffin	caribou	lobster
funeral procession	reindeer	crab
carriage	moose	often
wagon	threshing oxen	chased
sled	shark	some
chariot	bushel	nights
skunk	wolves	chasing
camel	salmon net	

Celestial Guidepost

follow me
I will
shape you
the way
snow makes
a cast
of silence

Ursa Major

Rarely slumps below the horizon but turns around and around the North Star as if making a bed for herself in leaves. Seven of her stars form the asterism The Big Dipper, or Starry Plough. The handle is the bear's tail, stretched from when Zeus threw her and their son into the sky. Though she is forever pinned to the north, for Van Gogh, the Great She Bear crawled through the blue night without black to the star-poor southwest and positioned her points to line up with the Arles streetlights reflected in the Rhône.

The Cosmic Hunt

One night a vision appeared to four hunters, brothers known for their skill at tracking quarry: a great bear was terrorizing a village, scaring away all the animals except for the ravens who stayed to clean up the bear's leftovers. Starving, the people hid inside their homes as the fire burned out in the village's center. The hunters, along with their dog, set off to kill the bear. Eventually they spotted her, but as if possessed by a deer, she ran swiftly through the forest. Bellowing their hunting cries, the brothers pursued the bear. As they closed in, it leapt off the earth and into the firmament. The hunters who followed are still visible chasing her through the night sky. In autumn, as the bear prepares to hibernate, they get close enough to shoot arrows into her body, and when they do, blood drips from the heavens onto the leaves of trees, painting them red, orange, and yellow. The arrows never kill the bear though her wounds make her unseen for some time. When she reemerges, the brothers continue their chase. Haudenosaunee lore offers various versions of the cosmic hunt, and other Indigenous Nations provide their own accounts. For instance, in some versions, the hunters are birds. The Mi'kmaq describe seven hunters who chase the bear: Chickadee, Robin, Moosebird, Pigeon, Blue Jay, Barred Owl, and Saw-Whet Owl. By autumn they begin to lose the trail and several of them quit the hunt. When the stars that form the Big Dipper's handle (Robin, Chickadee, and Moosebird) get close to the bear, Robin shoots it dead with an arrow and blood splatters the leaves of the maples and covers Robin in red. She shakes the blood off her body, but some remains on her breast. Eventually, the dead bear's fat covers the land in white and she is difficult to see by late November, for her skeleton lies low in the northern sky but her spirit returns to the den, represented by Corona Borealis. In some tales, when sap from the trees seeps into the womb of the underworld, the spirit of the celestial bear enters the body of an earthly bear and returns to the den to rest before beginning the cycle again in spring.

Funeral Procession

eighty-one light years

above this boiler
room   crawling along

the horizon
a bridge   over years

of trailing her
intently and blindly

this hunt a trial

this pilgrimage an escape

Ursus Arctos Horribilis

along a ridgeline an animal trail overlooking a valley

what's hued red in memory

locoweed lynx tracks bear scat

grinding your teeth is what you do

with the things you wrestled with before bed

hidden so well you can barely

hear them breathe

in the shade of the col

in your dreams

you chew roots and horsetails

Wrestle Can Mean Embrace

The wrestler sits alone on the berm with his thoughts in the night. The river below is so loud he doesn't hear the man approach. The man is an angel and the man is his worries and all the bad things he's done and the man is a god and everyone knows God is a bear. They wrestle through the night until the landscape begins to emerge from shadow: clouds, trees, trail, river, and then their faces. With a touch, the angel knocks the wrestler's hip socket out of joint but he doesn't quit. More determined, he pushes the angel's head into the dirt. "Let me go," God says, "for the day has broken." Before releasing him, the wrestler demands a blessing. A limp, a new name.

Instructions for Growing a Forest

To Grow a Forest

A marbled murrelet nests in the moss
of a decaying fir. Deadwood predators

sleep in the snags, shrubs and brambles
flourish in soil enriched by fear.

Ferns, fungi, saplings love trouble
at home. Forest seeds are dispersed

by wind and animal. A nutcracker carries
a hundred piñons in its sublingual pouch.

The wasps born inside the strangler
fig lug its seeds for miles. Their wingless

mother is with the Lord now. This is called
mutualism. The forest wants to travel.

The most effective dispersers of seed
with their leather satchels and warehouses

are humans. Using other forests, they spread
and cultivate their own: once there was

a little girl who lost her way in a dark
woods, or a poor woodcutter and his wife

abandoned their children in a wilderness.
The youngest, a tiny boy, no longer than

a thumb. A father, thinking he is giving away
one of his apple trees, is tricked into giving

his daughter to the devil and must cut off
her hands to protect her. To protect her

God sends an angel. A brother and sister,
discarded in backcountry, a cannibalistic

witch, a hut made of candy. Nothing nourishes
a forest like an absent father. Parental cruelty

is proportional to relative stand density of old
growth woodlands. A feckless uncle or jealous

stepmother yield biodiversity. The wood
welcomes disappointment, is home

to the endangered, for under a canopy
of tangled branches and scattered

openings in tall red cedars, she can
easily hide. Pricked by a fateful spindle

then the forest grows around a sleeping
child. *The thorns held fast together as if they*

*had hands, and the youths were caught
in them and could not get loose again.*

Punishment

the beauty of the devil's
back our mother loves
to tell us is blinding

We've Been Looking All in the Woods for Him

Her words scuttle through the landline to the dispatcher who thinks she hears the flute of a meadowlark in the background and remembers when, as a girl, she was lost in the gum swamp of the Neuse River. *What's the address?* she asks. *For the forest?* replies the grandmother. Canines, helicopters, local volunteers in their best boots, and law enforcement make a mess of the woods. They scour rugged terrain for the boy, but floods and freezing temperatures hamper their efforts. When the storm calms, they comb nearby ponds and rain-filled sinkholes. On the third day, the toddler is found tangled in thorn bushes, his fingers gleaming with frostbite. Later, he tells his aunt a bear took care of him. *God sent an angel.* Cherokee legend says long ago, not far from here, a child left his clan and was gone all day in the mountains. He returned but the next day ran off again. Defying his parents, over time, he stayed longer and longer away, until he no longer could take human food and his nature began to change, brown hair sprouting all over his body. Doesn't that sound sublime? The anticipation, the heart-pound of at last. Eventually the clan followed. To feel what it's like to be a bear is enough for an entire people to give up their humanness. Do they regret it? Beyond the strength in the back, balance, speed, besides the scent-defined world, smells like a brightness of colors if colors were noises, besides the courage, devotion, pitches known not even to dogs, is their shrinking habitat worth it? Do they forgive us, they who were once us? Imagine a forest after the rains and imagine the warmth of a love you've longed for, softly breathing. As the search team neared, they could hear the boy weeping. Were his cries because of the cold, the thorn scratches, or the fear of never seeing his mother again? Before she retreats into the heart of the forest, the bear embraces him. In this world you are loved and you will be wounded. Without sound she moves through thick brush still heavy with rain.

A Report on the Bear Wrestler

My dad wears a three-piece suit but when he's raking leaves he wears a flannel over a flannel and in the spring he cuts the sleeves off one of them and wears it like that. His arms look like the trunk of my favorite tree the one in front of our house. The gym guys call him Bicep Bob and his grandpa told him that he shouldn't go to college because with arms like that he should be digging ditches for a living. My dad is 6'4" the same height as Abraham Lincoln and Superman. His dad was 6'2" so my dad says I'm going to be 6'6." For my birthday party he dresses up as Superman and flies the boys through the house. We eat pizza and popcorn and watch Superman 1 and 2 and we start 3 but everyone falls asleep except for me. The bad temper Superman who blows out the Olympic torch and gets drunk at the bar looks like the vets we see downtown. One time my friend David jumped out the window while we were playing Superman like he really thought he could fly and he yelled Superman and broke his arm. Just like Superman my dad is a really fast runner. At the grocery store this guy stole my dad's briefcase and my dad chased him for a mile and caught him. My dad gets up at 4:30 almost every morning and runs ten miles. He sees a lot of animals on the road when he runs toward the airport. Once a deer followed him the whole time and then stood outside our house all day. He saw this dead girl on the road and had to call 911 and this other time he found this guy who was covered in leaves and my dad thought he was dead but when my dad checked his pulse he wasn't so my dad gave him mouth-to-mouth recitation and saved his life. My dad got sprayed by a skunk and had to run to the grocery store to buy milk to take a bath in. Two times when he was running he saw a bear. A long time ago when my dad was in the Navy he wrestled a bear and the bear threw him onto a hotdog stand. Sometimes he lets me put my finger in the scar on his back and

I can hear the bear growl but I know it's my dad pretending. My dad is super strong. When Don Reinhoudt the strongest man in the world came to Salvation Army Camp and did all these dumb things like ripping a phonebook in half I started to cry and when he let us ask questions I raised my hand and told him you're a liar you're not the strongest man in the world because my dad is the strongest man in the world and all the kids laughed at me and Don Reinhoudt said well I bet your dad is strong and maybe stronger than me but I won this contest a while ago and I interrupted him and screamed you're a liar you're a liar and everyone laughed and he got real quiet and looked at the counselors and then Don Reinhoudt asked me who my dad is and I said Bob Ostrom and he said oh wait Bob Ostrom I'm so sorry you're right I forgot he is the strongest man in the world and everyone shut up and he admitted that he was actually the second strongest man in the world. My dad can bend a penny with his bare hands. I look at his hands sometimes for a really long time. They're so cool. His hands are huge and dark and rough. When he's thinking he rubs them together and it sounds kind of like sandpaper mixed with the ocean inside a big seashell. The top of one of his middle fingers is gone. It looks like a bald man and my dad jokes that no one takes him seriously when he gives them the birdie. My dad lost his finger in a motorcycle accident. His girlfriend was on the back of the motorcycle and when they hit a curb she went flying over a fence but my dad's finger got stuck in the engine or something and when he was in the hospital the girl's dad came into my dad's room and punched him right in the face. Then a while after that my dad lost the same finger in a factory accident. I think they sewed it back on after the motorcycle crash but then it got chopped off again. When I came in from playing outside one day I found my dad on the brown flowery couch stitching a big cut in his arm. He had thread in his mouth and was pushing a needle through his bloody dark skin. This other time I accidentally left the side door open and when my dad pulled out of the driveway he grabbed the door and ripped it right off the house. My dad smokes a pipe and rubs it on his face to make it shine. Sometimes he quits smoking and this one time he threw his pipe against the garage wall and it shattered and scared the heck out of me. When my baseball team was in the playoffs and there were two outs in the bottom of the ninth inning and my coach didn't want me to bat my dad got really mad and threatened the coach and then the other parents yelled at my dad and he stood up and threw his coffee on the ground and held his hands up in the air and asked do any of you think you can take me. I struck out but I'm getting better. I want to be a gerontologist just like my dad. That's the study of aging but when I told Mrs. Jordan she thought I was talking about studying vaginas and sent me out into the hall. My dad knows the Reverend Billy Graham because he was on the Billy Graham Crusade and I went to see him on stage with Billy Graham. Before Christmas and on his birthday my dad gets cards from the president. He met Ronald Reagan and he had dinner with Barbara Bush but George wasn't there. On our way to Bar Harbor Maine we thought about stopping to see George Bush and his family in Kennebunkport but my dad said we probably shouldn't because of Iraq and the president is very busy. I really hope my dad runs for president. My dad isn't even a little bit selfish. If you like something he has he'll give it to you right away and he gets lots of people jobs. My dad works at an old folks home and brings back all these old coins for me and jewelry for my sisters. One time the boys were making fun of me and said I was on welfare and when I told my dad he got really mad and stormed out of the house I tried to stop him and then the next time I saw the boys they made fun of me because my dad has a PhD and then I got furious and Jimmy Barret who's really good at football kept saying Robbie's dad has a

PhD and I punched him like five times in the gut and nothing happened then he punched me once in the face and I spun and fell down and everyone laughed at me but then I pulled down his pants and ran home as fast as I could. Once when the boys came over to watch my dad lift weights Jimmy asked if he'll look like my dad someday and my dad said that most boys grow up to look like their own dads and Jimmy ran home crying because his dad is fat and bald. My dad is so handsome. He says it's a curse. He's the lead in all the community theater musicals and he sings really good. In my opinion his best role was Harold Hill in The Music Man. His second best was Jud in Oklahoma and my grandma and I cried when he died. My dad has curly hair but he sprays it down with Aqua Net so he looks just like Cary Grant but better and we have lots of Cary Grant books and movies and Cary Grant pictures in the basement. Upstairs we have a few paintings and a lot of mirrors and family photos but the frames are all missing glass.

False Awakening

a sliding door opens to the country   between the pond and an unlit pile
of trash my family   has a good time   did you just wake up someone yells
covered in mud   past my muck boots   between the barley   and the barn
one black bear then another walk in the direction of those   I love unaware
of the danger   always unaware fall is here   ripe fruit hang in dry leaves
the flock call of snow geese drown   the children's voices
my dad cuts his late daughter's hair   wisps fly toward the woods   the world
slides away from the sun   and when I run   my boots stay in the mud
the bears approach my cousins   I try to warn them   the stars the jewelweed
pods about to burst   not even my own blood can hear me in this place

Lily Dale Assembly

she chews her cuticles
as she steers with the other
hand past vineyards ruined
Victorians she says she saw
an egret on a tire pile there's
a space inside and all around her
and when you're in it what you
think are feathers is snow what
you think is snow are bones
between Fredonia and an urge
to raise a barrier to her own
desolation she slows to a stop
along the side of Route 60 the red
Pacer we call the spaceship smells
like cigarettes and maple syrup
barn music ringing in my head
my mother gave me ears
and sang into them a voice that
makes me feel she's all the spirit
I'll ever need I wait for her the way
we wait for the 8-track to click
*You see the lights of the town down
that hill* she points across my chest
and taps on the window I see it
at the base of the bank beneath us
Promise me you'll never go there
the asphalt salt-stained white makes
tonight seem bright despite the hour

without looking at me she says
That place is so crowded with spirits
you can stab the air with a needle she
gestures with one hand in the space
in front of me *and it will stick* when
I got stuck crawling in the caves
near Quaker Lake my body
trapped between rocks
my head forced to face the dark
was I still close enough to the day
I was born to know that where
I came from had to be better
than where I was headed I can't
recall how I got out but there's
a narrow hallway in sleep
with walls covered in ridges
of shells the bones of sea life
I can't force myself through or back
there were other prohibitions:
Ouija boards meditation lust
Dungeons and Dragons I never
told her about the talisman I kept
in my room and prayed to when
I was desperate or the day
was the face of an animal breaking
through the floor thirty years later
I break my promise I face the lake
and what surrounds me is what

always surrounds me: guilt
so thick it talks like a woodpile
I pray to my talisman to the spirits
to the frog and the shoreline in its eye
the mute swan hunting shiners
in the shallows but my blood
pulls me back this body always
making me aware of itself: wrong
life thin hide I try to say escape
but as if pushed from the cave of my
throat leaves and dirt fill my mouth trees
mirrored in Cassadaga Lakes like fire
on the water my body repeats her body
singing fire on the mountain each word
each day redesigns the landscape
of memory a little tree here a little
empathy on the shore I suck the pulp
through grape skins and sometimes
I spit the seeds into the mud
sometimes I chew them

To Grow a Forest

You can bury your body inside the hedges
by the front porch and trick yourself into
brambles: you have crept up to a woodland's
edge. Now stare into the trees and dream
of a mother bear suckling a human child.
You can even trudge along a blazed path,
imagine yourself running away from yourself.
But if you really want what you've been
wishing for, you have to walk off-trail
into the heart and meet what's been waiting
for you all your life. Pray it's well-fed
and that it slept through winter.

Exit, Pursued by a Bear

He went up from there to Bethel, and while he was going up on the way, some small boys came out of the city and jeered at him, saying, "Go up, you baldhead! Go up, you baldhead!" And he turned around, and when he saw them, he cursed them in the name of the Lord. And two she-bears came out of the woods and tore forty-two of the boys.

2 Kings 2:23-24

In the Shadow of Branches

after hunting fireflies

I had been working

my tongue into bark

I was not waiting for Him

nor did I call

it is by might I learned

love a taste like maple

then pine then needles

He made me let my body

be what it is

that was the other side

of tamed though owned

like hands cupping steam

did I feel anger I felt thirst

Where I Bury My Grief

she was weatherless

storms the woods

in winter

a sea without waves

she'd been wading

in drifts

led by an ancient breed

of dog was dogged

in deep snow here

The Yukon

to die like the tundra under your feet to find
out why you are always killing things in your sleep

I didn't bring you here for the bear
maybe you didn't even know you were here

under long shadows of white spruce across snow
you pry open the animal's mouth

how familiar these hands you think
and the tenderness with which it looks at you

turns your anger into itself and loose
on Azure Lake ice so thin a breeze shatters it

The Two She Bears

she had a blunt tooth divine purpose

the other was kept in

though they had always been together

looking back they know that

what began as light for a way

turned to wildfire overlapping

and laced as one voice

never interrupting but completing

did we kill them all

after that the clover lost its flavor

grass recovered from wind

like hackles a promise

a far-off storm taunting the spine

When Hunters Killed the Last of the Wolves

we lost our minds
        until then
        everything we loved everything
                even what we feared
                and who feared us
                as if leashed to one another

A Year End Rite to Drive Away Ghosts

epoch of swelling waters

keyed up typhoons when wild

berries shrivel under shadows

of dense pine in a time of vacant

streams glutted dams the summer

of quiet with fear in the year of stay

inside all the young city-bound

while the aging harvesters unable to bow

to the carrots or the shine muscats

that burst on the vine whose arms grow

weak in dusk from the weight

of apples red dragonflies wasps

rodents the dark woods hears

in a season of a paucity of acorns

a brown bear wades through a yellow

sea of canola blossoms toward

a garden beside a house beside

a farm our lives are honeyed

Cut from the Body Through Violence a Spirit Stays Near

my only wish

occupy me again

this time

without me

Killing of the Sacred

False Awakening

then I run
my hand
along the
nape to
the side
of my neck
where I
often feel
pity I touch
something
coarse like
guard hairs
like desert
grass on
a burial
mound
scabland
effigy
young sod
where years
ago a pond
in which
I swam

with catfish
and the mirror
carp
what swam
in me
unnamed
was always
dangerous

The Reincarnations of Mink the Bear

in my last dream as a man
I am a boy again

standing in the garage
with my granddad our

faces dirty from hulling
black walnuts by the forest

the old man hands me
a heavy sack of earth

and says lose everything
when I open it I find

the room where I sleep
my light my ceiling

my walls this life
is guesswork and nested

dreams in the next
give me hunger over

ease so I might know
what I want make me

a bloodhound buzzard
a dung beetle I want

to understand where I am
I have already been

practicing a celestial dance
in the yard

under the Milky Way
wake me up

in any swirling galaxy I
know now what it means

to be home the trees I feel
reaching inside of me

the ones I love my family
their roots covered in me

Treatment

It doesn't take long for me to find what I'm looking for
on YouTube: on a rocky shore on Vancouver Island
a black bear hunts crabs. I have arrived here out of
desperation. Most of this life I spent salting my own
earth. Calm and methodical the bear sniffs each stone.
The ease with which he lifts enormous algae-covered
rocks is soothing. He knows what he is doing. Crabs
waiting for the tide to return don't stand a chance.
In another video, crows follow close behind the bear
like pieces torn from his black coat. They clean up
scraps. Mountains in the near-still ocean. Music of
the bear chewing over the soft sound of small waves.
When I'm in the machine, I replay it in my mind,
imagine them in my spleen. Bear, crows, veins, bones.

The Kingdom

she was my skin my sky and earth
lived in the hollow of a fallen tree
I curled up on her belly beside my ghost
brother we nursed for months waited
for life to stir outside waited for the heather
cock the dormouse gray wolves and raven
cry at last spring came she taught me how
to climb a birch slept on my back in her soft
fur she on her back in the ferns drifting
off to the noise of a moose grazing alder
leaves we got into trouble my brother and me
tussled in the brush climbed into the window
of a deserted cabin matched paw to hand
prints in the dirt and watched mine fill with
rain back to home led by the scent of the sea
dinner was cowberries and a fistful of ants
laughing and lapping them off my arm
mother cradled me in her forelegs licked
my head though I was slow to find my feet
the day came when she chased me away
as much as I clamored she was resolute done
with me over time I ran to her less and less
and farther and farther to the edge of the forest
I strayed when the hunters found me my ghost
brother was up in a tree looking for honey
they took me to a city gave me a name a room

brought me to a man who pointed at me
then pushed his cold white finger to my brow
traced a cross oiled my chest poured water
on my head my ears my mouth the glamour
of evil he said created in your likeness he said
and on the skin of all the people there colored
by light through stained glass windows I saw
a shadow pass it made me bellow bark those
people shrieked all the water in the kingdom
of god couldn't wash the wild off me years
later I ran off just to taste the sap on a pine
when I turned around she was standing there
timeworn her fur tattered in places one paw
maimed her scent was home I knew then
I had never been and always will be alone

The Bear Wrestler

In his deep blue U.S. Navy bellbottoms, crackerjack, and white dixie cup hat, the young man ambles over moss-covered rocks to cross a wide stream, then up a bank. The evening sky is clear and, in the moonlight, the brick-red Virginia creeper and purple poison ivy mark the trail. He climbs up a ridge where dwarf pines turn him into a giant. From there, he looks farther into the forest and mistakes the canopy of a distant sugar maple for a bonfire. He rushes for its heat, down a slope, to the edge of a bog, where he grows miniature in the white cedars. It's darker here, and he senses that he's lost his way, so in the fallen cedar shoots he sits, gathers his thoughts, and rests his back against an outcropping of milky quartz. He starts to doze but is startled awake by something large panting in the woods. He convinces himself it's his own breathing. The relief quiets him and in that silence he hears the faint music of what he's been rambling toward. He jumps up and marches forward. As he nears, the woods echo the noise of laughter, screams, and carousel music competing with the bells of the high striker and crashes of the bottle stand. And as I reach that far back, I sense someone else is there, a younger boy in the trees, a ghost of myself. The boy is the emptiness between the trees and because he is thinner than ghost, his father who isn't his father yet doesn't seem to notice, though as if being chased, his pace turns to gallop. The rainbow glow of the funfair brightens the woods, but when he arrives, the only thing my dad sees is a boxing ring, surrounded by a string of colorful lightbulbs. At the center of the ring stands an enormous beast, a great brown bear. The bear calmly waits, sniffs the forest air. My dad spots his Navy buddies. They greet each other with back-slaps and jovial punches, and one of them asks, "How'd you get here, Bob?" Even as the woods swells around him, all that my dad can recall is walking along a neglected sidewalk to a parking lot.

The bear handler, a stout bearded man wearing suspenders over a dirty white t-shirt, with a long bullwhip on his shoulder, takes the stage. "Who among you possesses a heart uncorrupted? Who here is witless enough to step into the ring with the Lord of the Animals, cousin to the seal, the dog, the raccoon, Defender of the West, the Bee Wolf. Step not on its shit nor utter its name. Feared even by the Apache. Ursus Arctos. Neither beast nor human, God can whiff a white liver mountains away. One hundred greenbacks to the stouthearted fool who dares stay just thirty seconds inside the ropes with the Keeper of Dreams."

Egged on by his buddies, my dad waves his hat at the handler. Bets are waged. He takes off his jacket, hands it to a friend and climbs onto the mat. The bell rings and my dad starts to count the seconds. For the first five, the two stand there looking at each other. My dad can't distinguish the sound of his breathing from the bear's and he wonders at how small its eyes are. The bear starts toward him as if to greet him and my dad slowly edges along the ropes. "Nine, ten, eleven." The bear draws a long breath through its snout. My dad's clothes and hair, even the hairs on his arms, are drawn toward it. "Fourteen, fifteen, sixteen." Then the handler whips the bear on the rump. It stands on its hind legs and roars. At that moment my dad remembers the fiery maple he spotted hours ago. He stops counting and starts running. At the bear's every advance, my dad retreats, ducks and dodges. The audience jeers. The emptiness in the forest roots for his father. With a swat, the bear catches his sleeve, but my dad falls back, quickly crawls away and just then the bell rings three times. The bear sits. My dad starts to sidle out between the ropes, but the handler urges him back in, holds up my dad's arm, and waves a hundred dollar bill. Right before handing it to my dad, he looks at him and asks, "Double or nothing?" My dad pauses then slowly unbuttons his shirt and throws it out of the ring.

The second round is a different fight. My dad knows he can't outrun the bear anymore. When the bear lunges, my dad fakes right then sidesteps behind the animal. Instinctually, he wraps his long arms around its body. It's almost too easy and with his cheek pressed up against the bear's back, the irony of the hug moves my dad to grin at the audience. Something changes in the bear. My dad can feel its body swell, its fur darken to black. The bear's back begins to sear and though my dad wants to release it, he feels as if the bear is pulling him into the fire of its body. The horror of that heat draws from my dad sounds buried, a language forgotten but written in his blood. Upon hearing these grunts, as if to get a better look at his opponent, the bear shifts and rolls my dad off. He staggers across the ring, looks around and in his dizziness it seems every person in the audience is the same person. They all look a bit like him. Until now, the fight was rageless. But across from him, the bear stands taller and its intention is fixed. Again, it attacks my dad who thinks to dodge it but this time the bear has him before he can budge. It lifts him off his feet and, as if to force him to nurse, the bear buries my dad's face into the deep fur of its chest. The scent of the bear is unlike anything my dad has ever smelled. It's marvelous. My dad opens his mouth to taste summer wind in wild blueberry bushes. Farther into the bear, everything goes silent except for the faint sound of the cracking of his own bones. The sound conjures a cat walking across a mirror. The black cat becomes the black hair of a woman admiring her son. From everywhere on her body, hair reaches and my dad is gently wrapped in the long locks of her beard. It feels like love. He's floating downward in black waves when he sees streams of pink swimming past him. The wind that cools him is the breath of salmon. When he slowly settles to his back, a small house sparrow lands on his chin, puts its beak between my dad's lips and fills his mouth with cool spit. That's when my dad hears the most beautiful sounds: music of what ties the bear's muscles to its bones, to its tendons, and its bones to its bones. It seems to want to teach him something. It envelops my dad in the terror of his life so that he might pass through it. But my dad is not ready to travel that distance yet, so the bear pulls him away, and in that same motion, throws him out of the ring, toward a hotdog stand. How swiftly the bear replaces the weightlessness my dad just felt with momentum and gravity. Where he hits the stand, something cuts into his back and my dad feels his life gushing from him. As if a dam busted a mile away, water, red from dirt, rushes out of my dad. The lights, the ring, the cedars and their roots are washed away in a river of him. I see the bear and all the spectators spinning upwards, beating their arms and legs. There's a wild turkey, hundreds of bent pennies, colorful bottles, a fat decapitated finger, wrestling belt, Superman Underoos, corpse of a dog, a motorcycle. The water is filled with stories and water is the truth and the bear wrestler doesn't know how to swim.

NOTES

A History of Bear Wrestling in the United States

North American folk hero Daniel Boone was a renowned longhunter who contributed to the westward expansion of the United States. He is best known for killing bears. The many inscriptions that Boone left on trees after kills became known as "Boone Bear Trees," one of the country's earliest tourist attractions. *D. Boon cilled a bar in year 1760* takes its title from one of these inscriptions found on a beech tree in northeast Tennessee near the town of Jonesborough. Some years after the tree fell in a storm in the early 1900s, the Daughters of the American Revolution purchased the tree wood and had it made into tables, stools, sconces, candleholders, and as many as 500 gavels.

The language in *The Diary of William Bentley 1798* is lifted from Reverend William Bentley's writings. In July 1798, he noted that he "saw the young Greenland Bear in a Savage State," referring to a polar bear he saw on display in Boston.

Frontierland 1836: "King of the Wild Frontier" Davy Crockett claimed to have killed 105 bears in a single season.

Battling Bruno, Knight of the Royal Bath mid-19th Century: Battling Bruno was trained to entertain gold rush prospectors by engaging in boxing matches with other animals, including bears. He famously defeated "Gentleman Jim," a boxing bear from San Francisco, earning Bruno the attention of Queen Victoria who gave him the title Knight of the Royal Bath. Following his passing, Bruno was stuffed at the queen's request.

Les Montreurs d'ours d'Ercé 1870 and *Ursus Arctos 1871* came out of research done on the "montreur d'ours" or "displayer of bears," Pyrenees bear trainers who, from the mid-19th century until World War I, travelled the world. Some of the montreur d'ours eventually made a living as circus animal trainers in the United States. Ariege.com's article "The Bear Trainers of Ariège" and posts from the decedents of the montreur d'ours on the Circus Historical Society's discussion board were very helpful while exploring the history of these bear trainers.

Old Boy Martin 1871 is based on the bear training practices of the Usari and folk customs of the Romani people. The Romanian nursery rhyme "Dance, dance Old Boy Martin,/And I shall give you bread and olives!" finds its origins in a song once used by Usari trainers and perhaps part of a practice called "Old Boy Martin's Step" which involved having a bear step on a person's back to ensure fertility or ward away evil spirits.

Language in *Théâtre Français, New York City 1877* and the poem that follows was taken from an article in the December 20th, 1877 issue of the *New York Times* titled "Wresting Bears. Bauer and Regnier and their Antagonists—Bears that Force the Fighting and Bears that Evade it—the Men the Victors."

Lena's Revenge 1878: During a sharp rise in bear wrestling's popularity in the United States, a well-known bear named Lena wrestled Francis Borne in Troy, New York and, according to the *New York Times*, "was very roughly handled" by the bear. Although Borne was badly hurt, he did not seek medical attention for several weeks. From the same article, published on April 15th, 1878: "He also spat blood occasionally, but as there were no external marks of injuries, his friends did not believe he was seriously hurt. He continued to grow worse, however, and several days ago marks of the huge paws of the bear made their appearance on each side of his body…When an examination of the patient was made it was discovered that in his contest with the bear he had been terribly ruptured, and had received other internal injuries." Borne died in part due to the bear's handling of him though, as stated by the New York Deputy Coroner, the man's insides were "in a very bad condition, caused by fast living, and that he was also suffering from pyaemia…" In the October 25, 1976, *Sports Illustrated* article, "Bear Wrestling Took Hold 100 Years Ago, but Lost with Lena's Revenge," George Gipe chronicles the rise of bear wrestling in the U.S. in the late 19th and early 20th centuries and sees Borne's death as prompting its decline.

Bess at Roger's Park, Chicago 1902 uses language from *The Seattle Star*, February 25, 1902 found in the article "Barackman, Mervin (1894-1977) and His Wrestling Bears" by Peter Blecha. *Will You Miss Me When I'm Gone? Mervin Barackman 1930s* was also informed by Blecha's article.

Nick Lassa of the Oorang Indians National Football League Team 1922: Nicholas Lassa (1898-1964), a member of the Pend d'Oreille tribe, was born on the Flathead Reservation in Montana. He played guard for one of the NFL's original eighteen teams, the Oorang Indians, an all-Indigenous American football team formed by Walter Lingo, owner of the Oorang Dog Kennels. Lingo started the team to promote and sell his Airedale Terriers. The first-ever halftime shows are attributed to the Oorang Indians, who would put on performances and exhibit Lingo's dogs. During these shows, Lassa would often wrestle a bear.

Matilda the Hun 1980s is an erasure of an Andrew Sacher's 2021 *Vice* interview of Deanna Booher (aka Matilda the Hun, Queen Kong, Queen Adrena, Juicy Joy) titled "The Woman Who Wrestled Bears." After the California gaming commission barred women from wrestling men, Booher wrestled a seven-foot grizzly.

The archival information on nyprowrestling.com and wrestlingdata.com led to the discovery of various matches, bears, professional wrestlers, and original articles. I am grateful to the archivists who keep these records.

THE COSMIC HUNT

Much of the information in "The Cosmic Hunt" draws from Stansbury Hagar's article "The Celestial Bear" from *The Journal of American Folklore* published in 1900 and David Rockwell's *Giving Voice to Bear: North American Indian Myths, Rituals, and Images of the Bear*.

INSTRUCTIONS FOR GROWING A FOREST

"We've Been Looking All in the Woods for Him" was inspired by the story of Casey Hathaway, who at three years old went missing for three days in the North Carolina woods in 2019. After his rescue, Hathaway claimed he had been cared for by a bear. The poem was also informed by "Origin of the Bear" from James Mooney's *History, Myths, and Sacred Formulas of the Cherokees* found on the Northern Cherokee Nation website.

EXIT, PURSUED BY A BEAR

"Where I Bury My Grief" was sparked by the events surrounding the Sankebetsu brown bear incident.

News of bear encroachment and attacks in Japan due to global warming and depopulation along with a lack of the bear's natural predators (wolves went extinct in the early 20th century due to hunting, habitat loss, and disease) inspired

"A Year End Rite to Drive Away Ghost." This also prompted "When Hunters Killed the Last of the Wolves" which owes a debt to the November 11, 2020 *Reuters* article, "Japanese town deploys 'Monster Wolf' robots to deter wild bears" by Hideto Sakai, Akiko Okamoto, and Rocky Swift.

Killing of the Sacred

"The Reincarnations of Mink the Bear" draws inspiration from Mordicai Gerstein's *The Mountains of Tibet*. This poem is for Lisa, Rhea, and Wyatt.

"The Kingdom" is based on the late 17th century story of a feral boy found living with a Eurasian brown bear in the forests of Lithuania. This poem is for my mother.

The Bear Wrestler

"The Bear Wrestler" borrows from Norse mythology, especially from Gleipnir's Six Ingredients which formed the rope that binds the demon wolf Fenrir, otherwise known as "the deceiver."

ACKNOWLEDGMENTS

The years during which this book was written were difficult but would've been impossible, if not for the support of so many people. Thanks to my friends for conversations, encouragement, generous readings, and bear books: Pranav Behari, Diana Delgado, Timothy Hobbs, Greg Mertz, and Addie Palin. A special shoutout to Carey McHugh, Andrew Seguin, and Melissa Ostrom who have been with this project from the beginning. Without their unwavering attention and guidance, these poems would have been steered into the sands by ghost crabs and other distractions. For their collaborations, thanks to Robert Johanson and Aditi Kini. I am grateful to have had the opportunity to work with Nathan Catlin whose efforts to create cover art for this book helped me understand it more deeply. Thanks to my dad who is always ready to retell his stories and reminisce. And to those who helped sustain me emotionally and physically during the writing of this book: Hannah Hahn, Paul Hamlin, Caroline Hellman, Gerard Hellman, Anastasia Martinova, Amory Novoselac, Jennifer Oh, Sifu Henry Moy Yee, and my Moy Yee San Jong family. As always, I am grateful to my students and colleagues at New York City College of Technology. For allowing me to set up a writing space in the boiler room where much of this book was written, I thank my landlords, Piotr Lesniewski and Sebastian Siedlecki. Heartfelt gratitude to the Saturnalia family, especially to Timothy Liu for his friendship and editorial eye. And to Robin Vuchnich for her design work. Thanks to the editors of *The Bennington Review*, *The Ocean State Review*, and *The Poets of Queens 2* Anthology for publishing some of these poems.

I gratefully acknowledge the Lenape Nation, particularly the Mespeatches and Canarsee peoples, on whose ancestral homeland this book was written. Throughout history, Indigenous communities around the world have maintained a profound and interconnected relationship with bears. They have coexisted with bears: learning from, respecting, and sharing resources and land. Robust bear populations play a vital role in supporting the wider ecosystem; however, global warming and habitat fragmentation due to human encroachment have threatened this intricate web of connections. The endangerment of bear populations poses a direct threat to humans as well. By recognizing and learning from Indigenous wisdom, we can understand the importance of restoring Native lands to their original caretakers.

Finally, for building a life with me and making space for this project (not to mention all the bear stuff I have amassed), my deepest appreciation to my love, Lisa Jee, and our children, Rhea and Wyatt, who light the way.

ABOUT THE AUTHOR

Robert Ostrom lives in Queens, New York, with his partner, their two children, and two dogs.

Also by Robert Ostrom

The Youngest Butcher in Illinois

Ritual and Bit

Sandhour

The Bear Wrestler was printed in Adobe Garamond Pro
www.saturnaliabooks.org

www.ingramcontent.com/pod-product-compliance
Lightning Source LLC
Chambersburg PA
CBHW030527080526
44586CB00011B/344